Adobe Bridge CC
Keyboard Shortcuts

By

U. C-Abel Books.

All Rights Reserved

First Edition: 2017

ISBN-13: 978-1543228236
ISBN-10: 1543228232

Published by U. C-Abel Books.

Table of Contents

Acknowledgement.

All thanks to God Almighty for enabling us to bring this work to this point. He is a wonder indeed.

We want to specially appreciate the great company called Adobe Systems Inc. for their hard work and style of reasoning when it comes to providing the public with helpful programs and resources, and for helping us with some of the tips and keyboard shortcuts included in this book.

Dedication

The dedication of this book goes to every user
of Adobe Bridge CC.

How We Began.

W e enjoy using shortcuts because they set us on a high plane that astonishes people around us when we work with them. As wonderful shortcuts users, the worst eyesore we witness in computer operation is to see somebody sluggishly struggling to execute a task through mouse usage when in actual sense shortcuts will help to save that person time. Most people have asked us to help them with a list of keyboard shortcuts that can make them work as smartly as we do and that drove us into research to broaden our knowledge and truly help them as they demanded, that is the reason for the existence of this book. It is a great tool for lovers of shortcuts, and those who want to join the group.

Most times the things we love don't come by easily. It is our love for keyboard shortcuts that made us to bear long sleepless nights like owls just to make sure we get the best out of it, and it is the best we got that we are sharing with you in this book. You cannot be the same at computing after reading this book. The time you entrusted to our care is an expensive possession and we promise not to mess it up.

Thank you.

What to Know Before You Begin.

General Notes.

1. Most of the keyboard shortcuts you will see in this book refer to the U.S. keyboard layout. Keys for other layouts might not correspond exactly to the keys on a U.S. keyboard. Keyboard shortcuts for laptop computers might also differ.

2. It is important to note that when using shortcuts to perform any command, you should make sure the target area is active, if not, you may get a wrong result. Example, if you want to highlight all texts you must make sure the text field is active and if an object, make sure the object area is active. The active area is always known by the location where the cursor of your computer blinks.

3. On a Mac keyboard, the Command key is denoted with the ⌘symbol.

4. If a function key doesn't work on your Mac as you expect it to, press the Fn key in addition to the function key. If you don't want to press the Fn key every time, you can change your Apple system preferences.

5. The plus (+) sign that comes in the middle of keyboard shortcuts simply means the keys are

meant to be combined or held down together not to be added as one of the shortcut keys. In a case where plus sign is needed; it will be duplicated (++).

6. Many keyboards assign special functions to function keys, by default. To use the function key for other purposes, you have to press Fn+the function key.

7. For keyboard shortcuts in which you press one key immediately followed by another key, the keys are separated by a comma (,).

8. For chapters that have more than one topic, search for "A fresh topic" to see the beginning of a topic, and "End of Topic" to see the end of a topic.

9. It is also important to note that the keyboard shortcuts, tips, and techniques listed in this book are for users of Adobe Bridge CC.

10. To get more information on this title visit ucabelbooks.wordpress.com and search the site using keywords related to it.

11. Our chief website is under construction.

Some Short Forms You Will Find in This Book and Their Full Meaning.

Here are short forms used in this Adobe Bridge CC Keyboard Shortcuts book and their full meaning.

1.	Win	-	Windows logo key
2.	Tab	-	Tabulate Key
3.	Shft	-	Shift Key
4.	Prt sc	-	Print Screen
5.	Num Lock	-	Number Lock Key
6.	F	-	Function Key
7.	Esc	-	Escape Key
8.	Ctrl	-	Control Key
9.	Caps Lock	-	Caps Lock Key
10.	Alt	-	Alternate Key

CHAPTER 1.

Fundamental Knowledge of Keyboard Shortcuts.

Without the existence of the keyboard, there wouldn't have been anything like keyboard shortcuts so in this chapter we will learn a little about the computer keyboard before moving to keyboard shortcuts.

1. Definition of Computer Keyboard.

This is an input device that is used to send data to computer memory.

Sketch of a Keyboard

1.1 Types of Keyboard.

  i. Standard (Basic) Keyboard.
  ii. Enhanced (Extended) Keyboard.

  i. **Standard Keyboard:** This is a keyboard designed during the 1800s for mechanical typewriters with just 10 function keys (F keys) placed at the left side of it.

  ii. **Enhanced Keyboard:** This is the current 101 to 102-key keyboard that is included in almost all the personal computers (PCs) of nowadays, which has 12 function keys, usually at the top side of it.

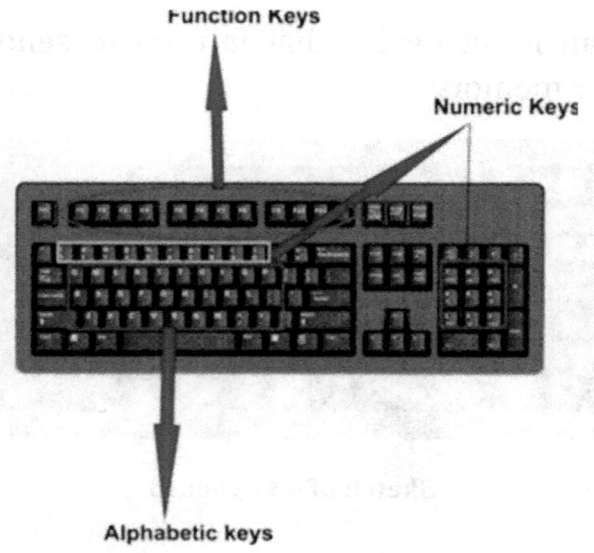

Function Keys

Numeric Keys

Alphabetic keys

1.2 Segments of the keyboard

- Numeric keys.
- Alphabetic keys.
- Punctuation keys.
- Windows Logo key.
- Function keys.
- Special keys.

Numeric Keys: Numeric keys are keys with numbers from **0 - 9**.

Alphabetic Keys: These are keys that have alphabets on them, ranging from **A** to **Z**.

Punctuation Keys: These are keys of the keyboard used for punctuation, examples include comma, full stop, colon, question marks, hyphen, etc.

Windows Logo Key: A key on Microsoft Computer keyboard with its logo displayed on it. Search for this ⊞ on your keyboard.

Apple Key: This also known as Command key is a modifier key that you can find on an Apple keyboard. It usually has the image of an apple or command logo on it. Search for this on your Apple keyboard ⌘

Function Keys: These are keys that have **F** on them which are usually combined with other keys. They are F1 - F12, and are also in the class called *Special Keys*.

Special Keys: These are keys that perform special functions. They include: Tab, Ctrl, Caps lock, Insert, Prt sc, alt gr, Shift, Home, Num lock, Esc, and many others. Special keys differ according to the type of computer involved. In some keyboard layout, especially laptops, the keys that turn the speaker on/off, the one that increases/decreases volume, the key that turns the computer Wifi on/off are also special keys.

Other Special Keys Worthy of Note.

Enter Key: This is located at the right-hand corner of most keyboards. It is used to send messages to the computer to execute commands, in most cases it is used to mean "Ok" or "Go".

Escape Key (ESC): This is the first key on the upper left of most keyboards. It is used to cancel routines, close menus and select options such as **Save** according to circumstances.

Control Key (CTRL): It is located on the bottom row of the left and right hand side of the keyboard. They also work with the function keys to execute commands using Keyboard shortcuts (key combinations).

Alternate Key (ALT): It is located on the bottom row also of some keyboard, very close to the CTRL key on both side of the keyboard. It enables many editing functions to be accomplished by using some keystroke combinations on the keyboard.

Shift Key: This adds to the roles of function keys. In addition, it enables the use of alternative function of a particular button (key), especially, those with more than one function on a key. E.g. use of capital letters, symbols, and numbers.

1.3. Selecting/Highlighting With Keyboard.

This is a highlighting method or style where data is selected using the computer keyboard instead of a computer mouse.

To do this:

- Move your cursor to the text or object you want to highlight, make sure that area is active,
- Hold down the shift key with one finger,
- Then use another finger to move the arrow key that points to the direction you want to highlight.

1.4 The Operating Modes Of The Keyboard.

Just like the computer mouse, keyboard has two operating modes. The two modes are Text Entering Mode and Command Mode.

a. **Text Entering Mode:** this mode gives the operator/user the opportunity to type text.
b. **Command Mode:** this is used to command the operating system/software/application to execute commands in certain ways.

2. Ways To Improve In Your Typing Skill.

1. Put Your Eyes Off The Keyboard.

This is the aspect of keyboard usage that many don't find funny because they always ask. "How can I put my eyes off the keyboard when I am running away from the occurrence of errors on my file?" My aim is to be fast, is this not going to slow me down?

Of course, there will be errors and at the same time your speed will slow down but the motive behind the introduction to this method is to make you faster than you are. Looking at your keyboard while you type can make you get a sore neck, it is better you learn to touch type because the more you type with your eyes fixed on the screen instead of the keyboard, the faster you become.

An alternative to keeping your eyes off your keyboard is to use the *"Das Keyboard Ultimate"*.

2. Errors Challenge You

It is better to fail than to not try at all. Not trying at all is an attribute of the weak and lazybones. When you make mistakes, try again because errors are opportunities for improvement.

3. Good Posture (Position Yourself Well).

Do not adopt an awkward position while typing. You should get everything on your desk organized or arranged before sitting to type. Your posture while typing contributes to your speed and productivity.

4. Practice

Here is the conclusion of everything said above. You have to practice your shortcuts constantly. The practice alone is a way of improvement. "Practice brings improvement". Practice always.

2.1 Software That Will Help You Improve Your Typing Skill.

There are several Software programs for typing that both kids and adults can use for their typing skill. Here is a list of software that can help you improve in your typing: Mavis Beacon, Typing Instructor, Mucky Typing Adventure, Rapid Tying Tutor, Letter Chase Tying Tutor, Alice Touch Typing Tutor and many more. Personally, I love Mavis Beacon.

To learn typing using MAVIS BEACON, install Mavis Beacon software to your computer, start with keyboard lesson, then move to games. Games like **Penguin Crossing, Creature Lab**, or **Space Junk** will help you become a professional in typing. Typing and keyboard shortcuts work hand-in-hand.

Sketch of a computer mouse

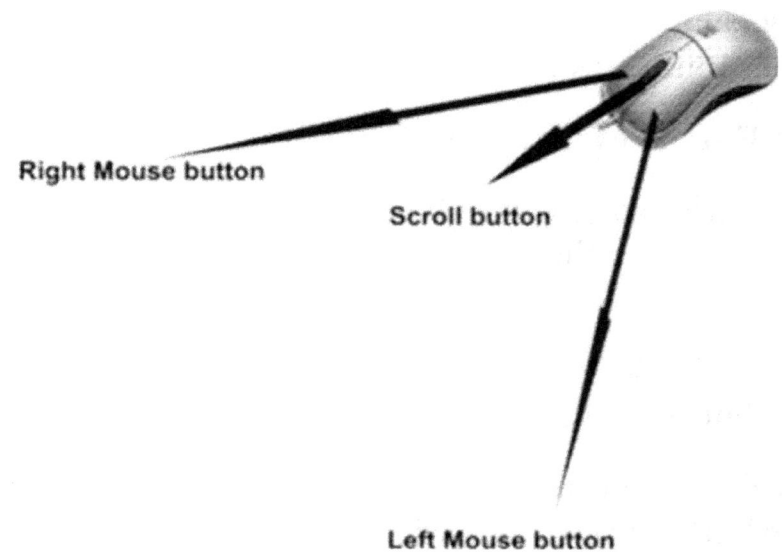

Right Mouse button

Scroll button

Left Mouse button

3. Mouse:

This is an oval-shaped portable input device with three buttons for scrolling, left clicking, and right clicking that enables work to be done effectively on a computer. The plural form of mouse is mice.

3.1 Types of Computer Mouse

- Mechanical Mouse.
- Optical Mechanical Mouse (Optomechanical).
- Laser Mouse.

- Optical Mouse.
- BlueTrack Mouse.

3.2 Forms of Clicking:

Left Clicking: This is the process of clicking the left side button of the mouse. It can also be called *clicking* without the addition of *left*.

Right Clicking: It is the process of clicking the right side button of a computer mouse.

Double Clicking: It is the process of clicking the left side button two times (twice) and immediately.

Triple Clicking: It is the process of clicking the left side button three times (thrice) and immediately.

Double clicking is used to select a word while triple clicking is used to select a sentence or paragraph.

Scroll Button: It is the little key attached to the mouse that looks like a tiny wheel. It takes you up and down a page when moved.

3.3 Mouse Pad: This is a small soft mat that is placed under the mouse to make it have a free movement.

3.4 Laptop Mouse Touchpad

This unlike the mouse we explained above is not external, rather it is inbuilt (comes with the laptop computer). With the presence of a laptop mouse touchpad, an external mouse is not needed to use a laptop, except in a case where it is malfunctioning or the operator prefers to use external one for some reasons.

The laptop mouse touchpad is usually positioned at the end of the keyboard section of a laptop computer. It is rectangular in shape with two buttons positioned below it. The two buttons/keys are used for left and right clicking just like the external mouse. Some laptops come with four mouse keys. Two placed above the mouse for left and right clicking and two other keys placed below it for the same function.

4. Definition Of Keyboard Shortcuts.

Keyboard shortcuts are defined as a series of keys, most times with combination that execute tasks which typically involve the use of mouse or other input devices.

5. Why You Should Use Shortcuts.

1. One may not be able to use a computer mouse easily because of disability or pain.

2. One may not be able to see the mouse pointer as a result of vision impairment, in such case what will the person do? The answer is SHORTCUT.

3. Research has made it known that Extensive mouse usage is related to Repetitive Syndrome Injury (RSI) greatly than the use of keyboard.

4. Keyboard shortcuts speed up computer users, making learning them a worthwhile effort.

5. When performing a job that requires precision, it is wise that you use the keyboard instead of mouse, for instance, if you are dealing with Text Editing, it is better you handle it using keyboard shortcuts than spending more time doing it with your computer mouse alone.

6. Studies calculate that using keyboard shortcuts allows working 10 times faster than working with the mouse. The time you spend looking for the mouse and then getting the cursor to the position you want is lost! Reducing your work duration by 10 times gives you greater results.

5.1 Ways To Become A Lover Of Shortcuts.

1. Always have the urge to learn new shortcut keys associated with the programs you use.
2. Be happy whenever you learn a new shortcut.

3. Try as much as you can to apply the new shortcuts you learnt.
4. Always bear it in mind that learning new shortcuts is worth it.
5. Always remember that the use of keyboard shortcuts keeps people healthy while performing computer activities.

5.2 How To Learn New Shortcut Keys
1. Do a research on them: quick references (a cheat sheet comprehensively compiled like ours) can go a long way to help you improve.
2. Buy applications that show you keyboard shortcuts every time you execute an action with mouse.
3. Disconnect your mouse if you must learn this fast.
4. Read user manuals and help topics (Whether offline or online).

5.3 Your Reward For Knowing Shortcut Keys.
1. You will get faster unimaginably.
2. Your level of efficiency will increase.
3. You will find it easy to use.
4. Opportunities are high that you will become an expert in what you do.
5. You won't have to go for **Office button**, click **New,** click **Blank and Recent**, and click **Create**

just to insert a fresh/blank page. **Ctrl +N** takes care of that in a second.

A Funny Note: Keyboarding and Mousing are in a marital union with Keyboarding being the head, so it will be unfair for anybody to put asunder between them.

5.4 Why We Emphasize On The Use of Shortcuts.

You may never leave your mouse completely unless you are ready to make your brain a box of keyboard shortcuts which will really be frustrating, just imagine yourself learning all shortcuts that go with the programs you use and their various versions. You shouldn't learn keyboard shortcuts that way.

Why we are emphasizing on the use of shortcuts is because mouse usage is becoming unusually common and unhealthy, too. So we just want to make sure both are combined so you can get fast, productive and healthy in your computer activities. All you need to know is just the most important ones associated with the programs you use.

CHAPTER 2.

15 (Fifteen) Special Keyboard Shortcuts.

The fifteen special keyboard shortcuts are fifteen (15) shortcuts every computer user should know.

The following is a list of keyboard shortcuts every computer user should know:

1. **Ctrl + A:** Control A, highlights or selects everything you have in the environment where you are working.

    *If you are like **"Wow, the content of this document is large and there is no time to select all of it, besides, it's going to mount pressure on my computer?"** Using the mouse for this is an outdated method of handling a task like selecting all, Ctrl+A will take care of that in a second.*

2. **Ctrl + C:** Control C copies any highlighted or selected element within the work environment.

   Saves the time and stress which would have been used to right click and click again just to copy. Use ctrl+c.

3. **Ctrl + N:** Control N opens a new window or file.

   Instead of clicking **File, New, blank/ template** *and another* **click,** *just press* **Ctrl + N** *and a fresh page or window will appear instantly.*

4. **Ctrl + O:** Control O opens a new program.

   Use ctrl +O when you want to locate / open a file or program.

5. **Ctrl + P:** Control P prints the active document.

   Always use this to locate the printer dialog box, and thereafter print.

6. **Ctrl + S:** Control S saves a new document or file and changes made by the user.

   Please stop! Don't use the mouse. Just press Ctrl+S and everything will be saved.

7. **Ctrl +V:** Control V pastes copied elements into the active area of the program in use.

Using ctrl+V in a case like this Saves the time and stress of right clicking and clicking again just to paste.

8. **Ctrl + W:** Control W is used to close the page you are working on when you want to leave the work environment.

> **"There is a way Debby does this without using the mouse. Oh my God, why didn't I learn it then?"** Don't worry, I have the answer. Debby presses Ctrl+W to close active windows.

9. **Ctrl + X:** Control X cuts elements (making the elements to disappear from their original place). The difference between cutting and deleting elements is that in Cutting, what was cut doesn't get lost permanently but prepares itself so that it can be pasted on another location defined by the user.

> *Use ctrl+x when you think **"this shouldn't be here and I can't stand the stress of retyping or redesigning it on the rightful place it belongs".***

10. **Ctrl + Y:** Control Y undoes already done actions.

> *Ctrl+Z brought back what you didn't need? Press Ctrl+ Y to remove it again.*

11. **Ctrl + Z:** Control Z redoes actions.
Can't find what you typed now or a picture you inserted, it suddenly disappeared or you mistakenly removed it? Press Ctrl+Z to bring it back.

12. **Alt + F4:** Alternative F4 closes active windows or items.

    *You don't need to move the mouse in order to close an active window, just press **Alt + F4**. Also use it when you are done or you don't want somebody who is coming to see what you are doing.*

13. **Ctrl + F6:** Control F6 Navigates between open windows, making it possible for a user to see what is happening in windows that are active.
Are you working in Microsoft Word and want to find out if the other active window where your browser is loading a page is still progressing? Use Ctrl + F6.

14. **F1:** This displays the help window.

    *Is your computer malfunctioning? Use **F1** to find help when you don't know what next to do.*

15. **F12:** This enables user to make changes to an already saved document.

    F12 is the shortcut to use when you want to change the format in which you saved your existing document, password it, change its name, change the file location or destination, or make other changes to it. It will save you time.

Note: The Control (Ctrl) key on Windows and Linux operating system is the same thing as Command (Cmmd) key on a Macintosh computer. So if you replace Control with Command key on a Mac computer for the special shortcuts listed above, you will get the same result.

CHAPTER 3.

Tips, Techniques, and Keyboard Shortcuts for use in Adobe Bridge.

About the application: It is a great media manager for visual people, developed and sold by adobe Systems Incorporated.

A fresh topic

Adobe Bridge Workspace.

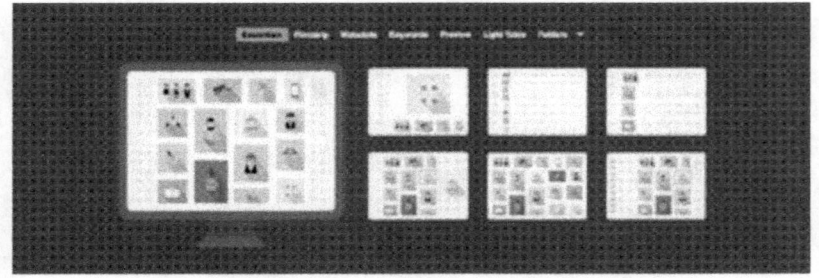

Workspace Overview.

The Adobe Bridge workspace consists of three columns, or panes, that contain various panels. You can adjust the Adobe Bridge workspace by moving or resizing panels. You can create custom workspaces or select from several preconfigured Adobe Bridge workspaces.

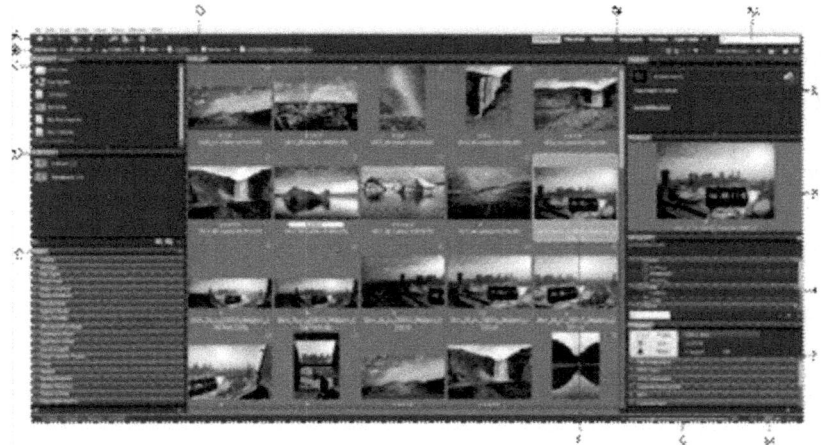

Adobe Bridge workspace

A. Application bar **B.** Path bar **C.** Favorites panel & Folders panel (tabbed) **D.** Collections panel **E.** Filter panel **F.** Selected item **G.** Thumbnail slider **H.** View options **I.** Metadata panel **J.** Keywords panel **K.** Preview panel **L.** Publish panel **M.** Quick Search box **N.** Standard workspaces **O.** Content panel

The following are the main components of the Adobe Bridge workspace:

Application bar

Provides buttons for essential tasks, such as navigating the folder hierarchy, switching workspaces, and searching for files.

Path bar

Shows the path for the folder you're viewing and allows you to navigate the directory.

Favorites panel

Gives you quick access to frequently browsed folders.

Folders panel

Shows the folder hierarchy. Use it to navigate folders.

Filter panel

Lets you sort and filter files that appear in the Content panel.

Collections panel

Lets you create, locate, and open collections and smart collections.

Content panel

Displays files specified by the navigational menu buttons, Path bar, Favorites panel, Folders panel, or Collections panel.

Publish panel

Lets you upload photos to Adobe Stock from within the Bridge app. See <u>Publish images to Adobe Stock</u> for details.
To view this panel in any workspace, choose Window > Publish Panel.

Preview panel

Displays a preview of the selected file or files. Previews are separate from, and typically larger than, the thumbnail image displayed in the Content panel. You can reduce or enlarge the preview by resizing the panel.

Metadata panel

Contains metadata information for the selected file. If multiple files are selected, shared data (such as keywords, date created, and exposure setting) is listed.

Keywords panel

Helps you organize your images by attaching keywords to them.

Search Adobe Stock.

Introduced in Bridge CC 2017

In addition to searching for assets in Bridge or on your computer, you can also use the Quick Search box (on the right side of the Application bar) to search for high-quality Adobe Stock illustrations, vectors, and photos. When you search, the results appear on the Adobe Stock website in your default web browser.

To switch your search between Adobe Stock search and Windows (Win)/Spotlight (Mac) search options, use the drop-down list in the Quick Search box.

Adjust Panels.

You can adjust the Adobe Bridge window by moving and resizing its panels. However, you can't move panels outside the Adobe Bridge window.

- Do any of the following:
  - Drag a panel by its tab into another panel.
  - Drag the horizontal divider bar between panels to make them larger or smaller.
  - Drag the vertical divider bar between the panels and the Content panel to resize the panels or Content panel.

- o To show or hide all panels except the center panel, Press Tab (the center panel varies depending on the workspace you've chosen).
- o Choose Window, followed by the name of the panel you want to display or hide.
- o Right-click (Windows) or Control-click (Mac OS) a panel tab and choose the name of the panel you want to display.

Work with Favorites.

- To specify Favorites preferences, choose Edit > Preferences (Windows) or Adobe Bridge CC > Preferences (Mac OS). Click General, and select desired options in the Favorite Items area of the Preferences dialog box.
- To add items to Favorites, do one of the following:
  - o Drag a file or folder to the Favorites panel from Windows Explorer (Windows), the Finder (Mac OS), or the Content or Folders panel of Adobe Bridge.
  - o Select a file, folder, or collection in Adobe Bridge and choose File > Add To Favorites.

Note:

To remove an item from the Favorites panel, select it and choose File > Remove From Favorite. Or right-click (Windows) or Control-click (Mac OS) the item and choose Remove From Favorites from the context menu.

Select and Manage Workspaces.

An Adobe Bridge workspace is a certain configuration or layout of panels. You can select either a preconfigured workspace or a custom workspace that you have previously saved.

By saving various Adobe Bridge workspaces, you can work in (and quickly switch between) different layouts. For example, use one workspace to sort new photos and another to work with footage files from an After Effects composition.

Adobe Bridge provides the following preconfigured workspaces:

Metadata

Displays the Content panel in List view, along with the Favorites, Metadata, Filter, and Export panels.

Essentials

Displays the Favorites, Folders, Filter, Collections, Export, Content, Preview, Metadata, and Keywords panels.

Filmstrip

Displays thumbnails in a scrolling horizontal row (in the Content panel) along with a preview of the currently selected item (in the Preview panel). Also displays the Favorites, Folders, Filter, Collections, and Export panels.

Keywords

Displays the Content panel in Details view, along with the Favorites, Keywords, Filter, and Export panels.

Note:

In Mac OS, pressing Command+F5 to load the Keywords workspace starts Mac OS voice-over by default. To load the Preview workspace by using the keyboard shortcut, first disable the voice-over shortcut in Mac OS Keyboard Shortcuts preferences. For instructions, see Mac OS Help.

Preview

Displays a large Preview panel; a narrow, vertical Content panel in Thumbnails view; and the Favorites, Folders, Filter, Collections, and Export panels.

Light Table

Displays only the Content panel. Files are displayed in Thumbnails view.

Folders

Displays the Content panel in Thumbnails view, along with the Favorites, Folders, and Export panels.

- To select a workspace, choose Window > Workspace, and then choose the desired workspace. Or, click one of the workspace buttons in the Adobe Bridge application bar.

Note:

Drag the vertical bar to the left of the workspace buttons to show more or fewer buttons. Drag the buttons to rearrange their order.

- To save the current layout as a workspace, choose Window > Workspace > New Workspace. In the New Workspace dialog box, enter a name for the workspace, specify options, and then click Save.
- To delete or restore a custom workspace, choose Window > Workspace, and then choose one of the following commands:

Delete Workspace

Deletes the saved workspace. Choose the workspace from the Workspace menu in the Delete Workspace dialog box, and click Delete.

Reset Workspace

Restores the currently selected saved workspace to its default settings.

Reset Standard Workspace

Restores the default settings for the Adobe pre-defined workspaces (Essentials, Output, and so on)

Adjust Brightness and Colors.

Brighten or darken the Adobe Bridge background and specify accent colors in General preferences. To open preferences, choose Edit > Preferences (Windows) or Adobe Bridge > Preferences (Mac OS).

- To brighten or darken the background, go to the General panel of the Preferences dialog box and do the following:
  - Drag the User Interface Brightness slider to make the Adobe Bridge background darker or lighter.
  - Drag the Image Backdrop slider to make the background of slideshows and of the Content and Preview panels darker or lighter.
- To specify accent colors, go to the General panel of the Preferences dialog box and choose a color from the Accent Color menu.

Manage Color.

In Adobe Bridge, the thumbnail quality determines whether color profile settings are used. High-quality thumbnails use color-profile settings, while quick thumbnails do not. In CS5 only, use the Advanced Preferences and the Options For Thumbnail Quality and Preview Generation button in the application bar to determine thumbnail quality.

If you are a Creative Cloud member or own Adobe Creative Suite, you can use Adobe Bridge to synchronize color settings across all color-managed apps and components. When you specify color settings using the Edit > Color Settings (Bridge CC) or Edit > Creative Suite Color Settings (Bridge CS) command, color settings are automatically synchronized. Synchronizing color settings ensures that colors look the same in all color-managed Adobe products.

Change Language Settings.

Adobe Bridge can display menus, options, and tool tips in multiple languages. You can also specify that Adobe Bridge use a specific language for keyboard shortcuts.

1. Choose Edit > Preferences (Windows) or Adobe Bridge > Preferences (Mac OS), and click Advanced.
2. Do either or both of the following:

- Choose a language from the Language menu to display menus, options, and tool tips in that language.
- Choose a language from the Keyboard menu to use that language keyboard configuration for keyboard shortcuts.
3. Click OK, and restart Adobe Bridge.

The new language takes effect the next time you start Adobe Bridge.

Enable Startup Scripts.

You can enable or disable startup scripts in Adobe Bridge preferences. Scripts listed vary depending on the Creative Suite® components you've installed. Disable startup scripts to improve performance or to resolve incompatibilities between scripts.

1. Choose Edit > Preferences (Windows) or Adobe Bridge > Preferences (Mac OS), and click Startup Scripts.
2. Do any of the following:
   - Select or deselect the desired scripts.
   - To enable or disable all scripts, click Enable All or Disable All.
   - Click Reveal My Startup Scripts to go to Adobe Bridge Startup Scripts folder on your hard drive.

HiDPI and Retina Display Support.

HiDPI monitors and Apple's Retina displays allow more pixels to be displayed on your screen. To take advantage of advancements in high-resolution display technologies, Adobe Bridge CC includes native support for high-resolution monitor displays running on Windows and Mac OS X (for example, the MacBook Pro with Retina display).

Bridge CC is aware of different monitor dots per inch (DPI) settings. When you are working on a HiDPI monitor set at a DPI of 150% or higher, Bridge's user interface automatically scales to 200% so that you continue to see sharp and clear UI elements, readable font size, and crisp icons across a wide variety of DPI display settings.

Note:

Bridge supports a minimum screen resolution of 2560 x 1600. Working on HiDPI monitors with screen resolution set below 2560 x 1600 truncates the Bridge user interface and some of the items may not fit on the screen.

User interface scaling preferences (Windows only)

With High DPI support enabled on Windows, the Bridge user interface scales to 200% on HiDPI monitors. However, Bridge also allows you to manually set the scaling preference:

1. Choose Edit > Preferences > Interface.
2. In the Preferences dialog, click Interface.

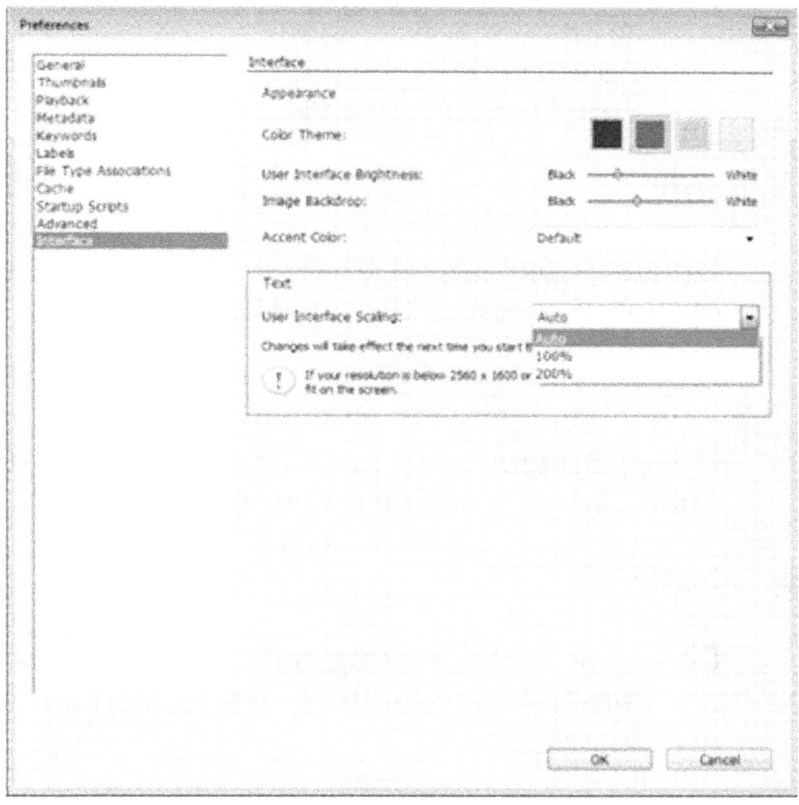

3. Select a User Interface Scaling option. You can choose any of the following:

Auto

(Default) Automatically scales the Bridge user interface to the following percentages based on the DPI setting of the display monitor:

- 200% at DPI >= 150%
- 100% at DPI < 150%

100%

Opens Bridge app at 100% scaling. Choose this option to revert to the pre-HiDPI look.

200%

Opens Bridge app at 200% scaling. Choose this option when working on HiDPI monitors.

Note:

Choosing 200% scaling option when working on non-HiDPI monitors truncates/cuts the user interface.

4. Click OK. Relaunch Bridge.

The scaling takes effect the next time you start Adobe Bridge.

Restore Preferences.

Numerous program settings are stored in the Adobe Bridge preferences file, including display, Adobe Photo Downloader, performance, and file-handling options.

Restoring preferences returns settings to their defaults and can often correct unusual application behavior.

1. Press and hold the Ctrl key (Windows) or the Option key (Mac OS) while starting Adobe Bridge.
2. In the Reset Settings dialog box, select one or more of the following options:

Reset Preferences

Returns preferences to their factory defaults. Some labels and ratings may be lost. Adobe Bridge creates a preferences file when it starts.

Purge Entire Thumbnail Cache

Purging the thumbnail cache can help if Adobe Bridge is not displaying thumbnails properly. Adobe Bridge re-creates the thumbnail cache when it starts.

Reset Standard Workspaces

Returns Adobe predefined workspaces to their factory default configurations.

3. Click OK, or click Cancel to open Adobe Bridge without resetting preferences.

End of Topic.

A fresh topic

Keyboard Shortcuts in Adobe Bridge CC.

Keyboard shortcuts let you quickly select tools and execute commands without using a menu. When available, the keyboard shortcut appears to the right of the command name in the menu.

Note:

In addition to using keyboard shortcuts, you can access many commands using context-sensitive menus. Context-sensitive menus display commands that are relevant to the active tool, selection, or panel. To display a context-sensitive menu, right-click (Windows) or Ctrl-click (Mac OS) an area.

This is not a complete list of keyboard shortcuts. This table primarily lists only those shortcuts that aren't displayed in menu commands or tool tips.

Use the following list of keyboard shortcuts to enhance your productivity in Adobe Bridge.

Result	Windows Shortcut	Mac OS Shortcut
Go to next view	Ctrl+\	Command+\
Go to previous view	Ctrl+Shift+\	Command+Shift+\
Show/hide panels	Tab	Tab
Switch between 0- and 1-star rating	Ctrl+'	Command+'
Increase thumbnail size	Ctrl+plus sign (+)	Command+plus sign (+)
Decrease thumbnail size	Ctrl+minus sign (-)	Command+minus sign (-)
Step thumbnail size up	Ctrl+Shift+plus sign (+)	Command+Shift+plus sign (+)

Step thumbnail size down	Ctrl+Shift+minus sign (-)	Command+Shift+minus sign (-)
Move up a folder (in Folders panel or a row)	Up Arrow	Up Arrow
Move down a folder (in Folders panel or a row)	Down Arrow	Down Arrow
Move up a level (in Folders panel)	Ctrl+Up Arrow	Command+Up Arrow
Move left one item	Left Arrow	Left Arrow
Move right one item	Right Arrow	Right Arrow
Move to the first item	Home	Home
Move to the last item	End	End
Add to selection (discontiguous)	Ctrl-click	Command-click

Refresh Contents panels	F5	F5
Add an item to the selection	Shift + Right Arrow, Left Arrow, Up Arrow, or Down Arrow	Shift + Right Arrow, Left Arrow, Up Arrow, or Down Arrow
Display Help	F1	Command+/
Rename next (with filename selected in Content panel)	Tab	Tab
Rename previous (with filename selected in Content panel)	Shift+Tab	Shift+Tab
Show items with star rating of 1-5 or higher in Filter panel	Ctrl+Alt+1 through 5	Command+Option+1 through 5
Show items with selected star	Ctrl+Alt+Shif t+1 through 5	Command+Option+S hift+1 through 5

rating in Filter panel		
Show items with labels 1-4 in Filter panel	Ctrl+Alt+6 through 9	Command+Option+6 through 9
Show all items with selected rating or higher in Filter panel	Shift-click	Shift-click
Clear filters	Ctrl+Alt+A	Command+Option+A
Select inverse in Filter panel	Alt-click	Option-click
Display Loupe tool in Preview panel or Review mode	Click	Click
Move Loupe tool	Click or drag	Click or drag
Display additional Loupes in Preview panel (multiple selection)	Click	Click

Move multiple Loupe tools simultaneou sly	Ctrl-click or Ctrl-drag	Command-click or Command-drag
Zoom in with Loupe tool	+	+
Zoom out with Loupe tool	-	-
Zoom in with Loupe tool (multiple selection)	Ctrl+plus sign (+)	Command+plus sign (+)
Zoom out with Loupe tool (multiple selection)	Ctrl+minus sign (-)	Command+minus sign (-)
Select all items in a stack	Alt-click	Option-click
Apply or remove current keyword and all parent keywords in	Shift-click	Shift-click

Keywords panel		
Forcibly remove current keyword in Keywords panel	Alt-click	Option-click
Open disclosure triangle in Keywords panel	Ctrl+Right Arrow	Command+Right Arrow
Close disclosure triangle in Keywords panel	Ctrl+Left Arrow	Command+Left Arrow

Applies to: *Adobe Bridge CC.*

Customer's Page.

This page is for customers who enjoyed Adobe Bridge CC Keyboard Shortcuts.

Our beloved and respectable reader, we thank you very much for your patronage. Please we will appreciate it more if you rate and review this book; that is if it was helpful to you. Thank you.

Download Our EBooks Today For Free.

In order to appreciate our customers, we have made some of our titles available at 0.00. They are totally free. Feel free to get a copy of the free titles.

Here are books we give to our customers free of charge:

(A) For Keyboard Shortcuts in Windows check:

Windows 7 Keyboard Shortcuts.

(B) For Keyboard Shortcuts in Office 2016 for Windows check:

Word 2016 Keyboard Shortcuts For Windows.

(C) For Keyboard Shortcuts in Office 2016 for Mac check:

OneNote 2016 Keyboard Shortcuts For Macintosh.

Follow this link to download any of the titles listed above for free.

Note: Feel free to download them from our website or your favorite bookstore today. Thank you.

Other Books By This Publisher.

Titles for single programs under Shortcut Matters Series are not part of this list.

S/N	Title	Series
Series A: Limits Breaking Quotes.		
1	Discover Your Key Christian Quotes	Limits Breaking Quotes
Series B: Shortcut Matters.		
1	Windows 7 Shortcuts	Shortcut Matters
2	Windows 7 Shortcuts & Tips	Shortcut Matters
3	Windows 8.1 Shortcuts	Shortcut Matters
4	Windows 10 Shortcut Keys	Shortcut Matters
5	Microsoft Office 2007 Keyboard Shortcuts For Windows.	Shortcut Matters
6	Microsoft Office 2010 Shortcuts For Windows.	Shortcut Matters
7	Microsoft Office 2013 Shortcuts For Windows.	Shortcut Matters
8	Microsoft Office 2016 Shortcuts For Windows.	Shortcut Matters
9	Microsoft Office 2016 Keyboard Shortcuts For Macintosh.	Shortcut Matters
10	Top 11 Adobe Programs Keyboard Shortcuts	Shortcut Matters
11	Top 10 Email Service Providers Keyboard Shortcuts	Shortcut Matters
12	Hot Corel Programs Keyboard Shortcuts	Shortcut Matters

13	Top 10 Browsers Keyboard Shortcuts	Shortcut Matters
14	Microsoft Browsers Keyboard Shortcuts.	Shortcut Matters
15	Popular Email Service Providers Keyboard Shortcuts	Shortcut Matters
16	Professional Video Editing with Keyboard Shortcuts.	Shortcut Matters
17	Popular Web Browsers Keyboard Shortcuts.	Shortcut Matters

Series C: Teach Yourself.

1	Teach Yourself Computer Fundamentals	Teach Yourself
2	Teach Yourself Computer Fundamentals Workbook	Teach Yourself

Series D: For Painless Publishing

1	Self-Publish it with CreateSpace.	For Painless Publishing
2	Where is my money? Now solved for Kindle and CreateSpace	For Painless Publishing
3	Describe it on Amazon	For Painless Publishing